PEOPLE YOU
SHOULD KNOW

ANNE FRANK

Get to Know the Girl Beyond Her Diary

by Kassandra Radomski

Consultant:
Harold Marcuse, Ph.D.
Department of History
University of California, Santa Barbara

CAPSTONE PRESS
a capstone imprint

Fact Finders Books are published by Capstone Press,
1710 Roe Crest Drive, North Mankato, Minnesota 56003
www.mycapstone.com

Library of Congress Cataloging-in-Publication Data
Library of Congress Cataloging-in-Publication data is available on
the Library of Congress Website.

ISBN 978-1-5435-5524-0 (library binding)
ISBN 978-1-5435-5923-1 (paperback)
ISBN 978-1-5435-5535-6 (eBook PDF)

Editorial Credits
Mari Bolte, editor; Kayla Rossow, designer; Svetlana Zhurkin, media researcher;
Tori Abraham, production specialist

Photo Credits
Alamy: Shawshots, 5, Sueddeutsche Zeitung Photo, 21; Bridgeman Images: UIG/Buyenlarge
Archive/Anne Frank (b/w photo), cover; Getty Images: AFP/Stan Honda, 11, Andrew Burton, 14,
Keystone-France/Gamma-Keystone, 27; Newscom: akg-images, 25, 29, Album/Fine Art Images, 8,
16, 17, Danita Delimont Photography/Sergio Pitamitz, 19, Everett Collection, 18, Heritage Images/
Fine Art Images, 6, 7, picture alliance/Archiv/Berliner Verlag, 13, picture alliance/Deutsche
Fotothek, 23, Zuma Press/Sunshine/AFS/AFF, 15; Shutterstock: Nejc Toporis, 28; SuperStock:
fototeca gilardi/Marka, 10
Design Elements by Shutterstock

Source Notes
p. 6, line 7: Anne Frank. *The Diary of a Young Girl*. New York: Doubleday, a division of Random House, 1967, p. 14.

p. 11, line 9: Anne Frank House. "How Welcome Were the Frank Family?" https://web.annefrank.org/en/Museum/Exhibitions/
Temporary-Exhibitions/Misschien-trekken-ook-wij-verder/How-welcome-were-the-Frank-family-in-the-Netherlands/. Accessed
8 May 2018.

p. 18, line 11: *The Diary of a Young Girl*, p. 112.

p. 21, sidebar, line 3: *The Diary of a Young Girl*, p. 85.

p. 22, line 8: Anne Frank House. "Tension and Arguments." http://web.annefrank.org/en/Anne-Frank/Not-outside-for-2-years/
Tension-and-arguments/. Accessed 21 May 2018.

p. 23, line 4: *The Diary of a Young Girl*, p. 240.

p. 25, sidebar, line 3: *The Diary of a Young Girl*, p. 245.

p. 28, line 9: *The Diary of a Young Girl*, p. 197.

Printed in the United States of America.
PA48

TABLE OF CONTENTS

1 THE LETTER

On July 5, 1942, a postal worker delivered a letter to a family in Holland. It was for 16-year-old Margot Frank. Inside was an order from Germany's Nazi Party. Margot was to report to a **labor camp** in Germany. A similar letter was sent to thousands of other Jewish people.

The Nazis considered Jewish people responsible for all the problems their nation had experienced after World War I (1914–1918). They decided that getting rid of Jews was the solution to the nation's **poverty**.

Margot's parents, Otto and Edith, were afraid. If Margot didn't report, the entire family, including 13-year-old Anne, could be arrested. Otto and Edith Frank believed the family had no other choice but to hide away the next morning.

labor camp—prison camp where prisoners are forced to perform hard work
poverty—the state of being poor or without money

Forced Labor

The first labor camps were organized in 1933 to hold people who opposed the Nazi Party. Soon more centers, called concentration camps, were built across Germany and countries it had invaded. The Nazis killed up to six million Jewish people during World War II (1939–1945), many of them in concentration camps. Others that the Nazis considered **inferior**, including Roma, people who were disabled, Jehovah's Witnesses, and gay people were also rounded up and taken to these camps. Prisoners were used as slaves and experienced brutal living conditions. After World War II began, the Nazis created death camps, where prisoners were worked to death or killed outright as soon as they arrived.

Jewish women and children arriving at Auschwitz-Birkenau, a concentration camp in Poland

inferior—lower in rank or status

The Franks had already arranged a hiding place. It was an empty space in the back of a building owned by Otto Frank's company. As the family rushed to pack, Anne worried. She did not yet know about the place she would later call the Secret **Annex**. In her diary, she wrote, "Into hiding—where would we go, in a town or the country, in a house or a cottage, when, how, where . . . "

Many of the Frank family's photos survived in an album hidden in the Annex.

annex—an addition or attachment to a building

Four family friends helped the Franks get ready to leave. They took many of the family's belongings to the hiding place that night. The Franks dressed in several layers of clothing. They could not pack suitcases for fear of being caught.

The next morning, Margot and one of the helpers, Miep Gies, left at 7 a.m. on their bicycles. Anne and her parents set off on foot about 30 minutes later. They walked through town for an hour until they reached their hiding place.

Today Anne's diary is displayed at the Anne Frank House in Amsterdam.

DID YOU KNOW?

Anne received a diary for her 13th birthday. She wrote to an imaginary friend she called Kitty. Her first entry was dated June 14, 1942, just three weeks before she went into hiding.

Anne (left), Edith, and
Margot in Germany, 1933

EARLY YEARS IN GERMANY

Anne was born in Frankfurt, Germany, on June 12, 1929. Her sister, Margot, was 3 years old. Otto was a businessman and Edith took care of the girls in their home in Frankfurt.

Life in Germany changed when the National **Socialist** Party, or Nazis, came into power in 1933. The country was heavily in **debt** after World War I. The Nazis, led by Adolf Hitler, blamed Jewish people for the poverty in Germany. Many people who did not like how the war had changed their lives believed him. Many Jewish people, including the Franks, decided they needed to get out of Germany. They feared—correctly—that their lives were in danger because of their religion.

DID YOU KNOW?

More than 8.5 million soldiers around the world fought and died during World War I. Even more civilians were killed. It is one of the deadliest wars ever fought.

socialism—an economic system in which the goods made by factories, businesses, and farms are controlled by everyone in society

debt—money that a person owes

9

2

ANNE'S DIARY

The Franks moved to Amsterdam in the Netherlands in 1933. The next year, Anne started school. She was smart and funny. Long before the family went into hiding, she told a teacher she wanted to be a writer.

Anne (center) at school in Amsterdam in 1937

Otto and Edith had hoped the Netherlands would stay out of the war. But the Nazis' power continued to reach across Europe.

On September 1, 1939, Germany **invaded** Poland. The following May, Germany invaded the Netherlands. The Franks tried to **immigrate** to the United States, Cuba, or England, but it was too late. Anyone with German ties was denied. "I believe that all Germany's Jews are looking around the world but can find nowhere to go," Edith wrote to a friend.

invade—to send armed forces into another country in order to take it over
immigrate—to come to live permanently in a foreign country

Anti-Jewish laws had already been passed in Germany. After being **occupied** by the Nazis, the Netherlands were put under the same laws. There were rules about where Jewish people could work and go to school. Books by Jewish authors were burned, and any Jewish-owned businesses were **boycotted**. Jewish people had to report their income and then had their properties seized. Anne and Margot were sent to a Jewish school, and Otto was no longer allowed to own a business. Jewish people had to wear a yellow star when they went outside.

The Franks decided hiding was the only way they could survive. Otto and his business partner, Hermann van Pels, who was also Jewish, began working on a hidden apartment. There would be enough room for both families.

occupy—to take possession or control by military invasion

boycott—to stop buying or using a product or service to show support for an idea or group of people

The Second World War Begins

Germany's invasion of Poland on September 1, 1939, started World War II. Great Britain and France declared war on Germany two days later. By mid–1941, Germany had invaded and conquered Denmark, Norway, Belgium, the Netherlands, Luxembourg, France, Yugoslavia, and Greece.

a sign reading "Forbidden for Jews" in the Netherlands, early 1940s

3

THE SECRET ANNEX

From the street, Otto's warehouse looked like a single house. In reality, it was two connected houses. The second house, where the secret apartment was, could not be seen from the street.

The first two floors of the building contained offices and a large warehouse. On the third floor was a short hallway that Victor Kugler, one of Otto's managers, used as an office. That office contained the only way to get into the back building, which Anne called the Annex.

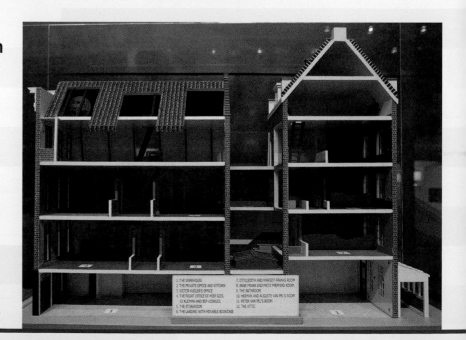

A model house showing the warehouse and secret apartment. The Annex is on the right side. The office with the entrance to the Annex is the small brown room in the center.

1. THE WAREHOUSE
2. THE PRIVATE OFFICE AND KITCHEN
3. VICTOR KUGLER'S OFFICE
4. THE FRONT OFFICE OF MIEP GIES, JO KLEIMAN AND BEP VOSKUIJL
5. THE STOREROOM
6. THE LANDING WITH MOVABLE BOOKCASE
7. OTTO, EDITH AND MARGOT FRANK'S ROOM
8. ANNE FRANK AND FRITZ PFEFFER'S ROOM
9. THE BATHROOM
10. HERMAN AND AUGUSTE VAN PEL'S ROOM
11. PETER VAN PEL'S ROOM
12. THE ATTIC

The Helpers

The five people who helped the Franks hide were Miep Gies, her husband Jan, Bep Voskuijl, Johannes Kleiman, and Victor Kugler. Anne called them the Helpers. They made sure the people hiding in the Annex had clothes, food, books, and news of the outside world. Although it was dangerous, they all immediately agreed to help. Jan, Jo, and Victor took over Otto's companies, allowing them to stay in business. Without the Helpers, hiding in the Annex would have been impossible.

Front row: Miep Gies, Otto Frank, and Bep Voskuijl. Back row: Johannes Kleiman and Victor Kugler.

DID YOU KNOW?

Bep Voskuijl's father, Johannes, was the warehouse manager. He built the bookcase to hide the secret door in August 1942.

The first floor of the Annex had been divided into two bedrooms that were shared by the Franks. There was also a small bathroom with a sink and toilet. The second floor of the Annex contained a kitchen that also served as a living room, study space, and bedroom. There was also a tiny bedroom at the foot of the stairs. The top floor was an attic space for storing food.

A week after the Franks' arrival, the van Pels family joined them. Hermann and Auguste slept in the kitchen space, while their 16-year-old son, Peter, slept under the stairs.

a photo of 14-year-old Peter van Pels

Fritz Pfeffer with his son, Werner, in 1932

The eighth and final Annex member arrived in November. Fritz Pfeffer was a friend of both families. He had sent his son to safety in England in 1938, and he and his Catholic fiancé, Charlotte, fled from Germany to Holland. However, by 1942 he realized he was no longer safe, and asked Miep if she could help him.

ANNEX LIFE

Life in the Annex was not easy. Sharing a tiny apartment with seven other people could cause arguments. They could not go outside, the windows were covered most of the time, and there was the constant fear of being found. Discovery meant they would be sent to a concentration camp and possibly to their deaths. In October 1943, Anne wrote, "The yells and screams, stamping and abuse—you can't possibly imagine it! . . . All this shouting and weeping and nervous tension are so unsettling and such a strain, that in the evening I drop onto my bed crying."

the outside of the office-warehouse where the Annex was located

But they tried to keep up a daily routine. They woke up around 7 a.m. and took turns using the bathroom. On weekdays, everyone had to be done using the bathroom by 8:30 a.m., when the workers arrived at the offices below. This was the most dangerous time of day. The Helpers did not arrive at the warehouse until 9 a.m. so any accidental noise could lead to discovery.

During work hours, everyone in the Annex had to be completely quiet. Anne, Margot, and Peter did schoolwork until lunchtime. The adults read, sewed, or worked in the kitchen preparing food for the next day.

At lunchtime the workers left the building. That was when one of the Helpers brought groceries and shared the day's news. After lunch, Anne and the others needed to be quiet for four more hours until the workers left for the night. They read or napped, and Anne wrote in her diary.

In the evenings and weekends, they could leave the Annex and go downstairs to the offices and the warehouse. They listened to the news on the radio. Anne and Margot danced and stretched, and they even did some office work for Miep. Each person got to take a bath in a wooden washtub once a week. But they could not go outside—ever. By 9 p.m., everyone had to return to the Annex to get ready for bed.

DID YOU KNOW?

The Dutch government fled to London after the Nazis conquered the Netherlands. During a radio broadcast, Anne heard the Dutch government ask those in hiding to save any diaries written during the war. Soon after, Anne began rewriting her diary entries on separate sheets of paper. She added some details for readers outside her family, and she took out some of her private thoughts.

A Heavy Load

Miep had to look hard to find enough food for everyone. She switched grocers often so the amount of food she bought wouldn't look suspicious. "Miep is just like a pack mule, she fetches and carries so much," Anne wrote. "Almost every day she manages to get hold of some vegetables for us and brings everything in shopping bags on her bicycle."

Miep and Jan Gies in 1957

Secret Names

Anne hoped her diary might be published someday, so she changed the names of the people in the Annex. Those pseudonyms would protect their privacy.

Anne struggled with her situation. She fought often with Fritz Pfeffer, the adult with whom she was forced to share a room. In her diary, Anne gave him the name "Albert Dussel." In German, Dussel means idiot. "It was clear right from the beginning that life in hiding would be far more difficult for the spirited Anne than for [the rest of] us," Otto said later.

Anne and the others hid in the Annex for two years. Bombings and air battles took place over their heads. Jewish people were rounded up and sent to concentration camps. Germany's forces took many losses as Allied troops and resistance movements fought back.

Several break-ins occurred. The Annex members could hear noises below but had no idea if it was someone searching for valuables, food, or people. "One day we laugh and see the funny side of the situation, but the next we are afraid, fear, suspense, and despair staring from our faces," Anne wrote in May 1944.

Between 1942 and 1944, more than 100,000 Jewish people living in the Netherlands were sent to concentration camps. Three-quarters of them would not survive the war.

4 ▷ CAPTURE

On the morning of August 4, 1944, members of the German secret police came to the office. They forced the helpers to lead them to the Annex.

The police searched the Annex and took any valuables they found. They dumped out the briefcase with Anne's diary and other writings on the floor so they could use it to haul away their loot. They did not find the family's photo album, which was probably hidden in an armchair.

After they left, Miep gathered up the papers and photos and put them away in her desk drawer. She planned to give them back to Anne when she returned. The armchair was probably sold to a family in Germany, who discovered the album many years later.

Miep kept Anne's diary, and 327 loose pages, safe until after the war.

D-Day

On June 6, 1944, more than 160,000 Allied troops invaded northern France. This day, which marked the beginning of the end of the war, is known as D-Day. "Hope is revived within us," Anne wrote. "It gives us fresh courage, and makes us strong again. . . . I have the feeling that friends are approaching." However it took another 11 months before the Allies could defeat the Germans and liberate the Netherlands.

The Franks, the van Pels, and Pfeffer were arrested. Four days later, on August 8, they were taken to Westerbork, a camp in the Netherlands. On September 2, they, and more than 1,000 other Jewish prisoners, were sent to Auschwitz, a concentration camp in Poland.

By this time, the war was nearly over. But it did not end soon enough. In late 1944 Mr. van Pels and Fritz Pfeffer died in concentration camps. Edith Frank died the following January. Peter van Pels and his mother died that spring.

Discovery or Betrayal?

For years people have wondered how the German police learned about the Annex. To this day, nobody knows for sure. There have been many theories, including:

- Wilhelm van Maaren, a replacement warehouse manager after Johannes Voskuijl fell ill, became suspicious. The people in the Annex noticed he set "traps" in the warehouse to catch people who were not supposed to be there.

- Someone who knew the family betrayed them. Possible suspects include a cleaning woman, a business partner or his wife, or a new employee.

Near the end of October or early November 1944, Anne and Margot were transported to Bergen-Belsen, a labor camp in northern Germany. They were there for more than three months. Survivors report that both girls were starving and became very sick with **typhus**. Less than two months before British Allied troops liberated the camp in April 1945, they died. Anne was 15 and Margot was 19.

Otto Frank was still alive at Auschwitz when the camp was **liberated** by Russian troops on January 27, 1945. He was the only one of the eight Annex members to survive.

Around 50,000 people died at Bergen-Belsen.

He learned of Edith's death on his way home. But there was no news of Anne or Margot. He asked other survivors and put ads in the newspaper. Finally he met sisters who had seen the girls in Bergen-Belsen before they died.

typhus—a severe disease that causes fever, headache, weakness, coughing, and a dark red rash
liberate—the act of freeing a person, group, or nation

a statue of Anne stands in Amsterdam

When Miep heard of Anne and Margot's deaths, she gave Anne's diaries to Otto. He was not able to bring himself to read them right away. But when he did, he was surprised by Anne's writings.

On April 4, 1944, four months before she and the others were found, Anne wrote: "I can shake off everything if I write; my sorrows disappear, my courage is reborn. But, and that is the great question, will I ever be able to write anything great, will I ever become a journalist or a writer?"

Otto honored Anne's wish and had her diary published in June 1947. It has since been translated into 70 languages, with more than 30 million copies sold. It has been made into several films and plays. Anne also wrote short stories, which were published as *Tales From the Secret Annex*. The Annex was turned into a museum in 1960.

Anne's words are a window into what it was like to live in hiding during World War II. They help people understand what it was like for Jewish people to be **persecuted** by the Nazis. Her diary also shows how brave some people are when they see horrible things happening to people around them.

Anne's optimism has inspired readers around the world.

persecute—to punish or treat badly for one's beliefs

GLOSSARY

annex (a-NEKS)—an addition or attachment to a building

boycott (BOY-kot)—to stop buying or using a product or service to show support for an idea or group of people

debt (DET)—money that a person owes

immigrate (IM-uh-grate)—to come to live permanently in a foreign country

inferior (in-FEER-ee-uhr)—lower in rank or status

invade (in-VADE)—to send armed forces into another country in order to take it over

labor camp (LAY-buhr KAMP)—prison camp where prisoners are forced to perform hard work

liberate (LIB-ur-ate)—the act of freeing a person, group, or nation

occupy (OK-yuh-pye)—to take possession or control by military invasion

persecute (PUR-suh-kyoot)—to punish or treat badly for one's beliefs

poverty (PAW-vuhr-tee)—the state of being poor or without money

socialism (SO-shul-is-uhm)—an economic system in which the goods made by factories, businesses, and farms are controlled by everyone in society

READ MORE

Bell, Samantha S. *Children in the Holocaust*. Children in History. Mendota Heights, Minn.: Focus Readers, 2018.

Folman, Ari, ed. *Anne Frank's Diary: The Graphic Novel*. New York: Pantheon Books, 2018.

Frank, Anne. *Tales From the Secret Annex*. Garden City, N.Y.: Doubleday, 1984.

INTERNET SITES

Use FactHound to find Internet sites related to this book.

Visit *www.facthound.com*

Just type in 9781543555240 and go.

 Check out projects, games and lots more at
www.capstonekids.com

CRITICAL THINKING QUESTIONS

1. Which parts of Anne's time in hiding do you think were the easiest—or hardest—to prepare for, and why?

2. Why was it so important for the residents in the Annex to stay quiet? Describe a time when you had to be extremely cautious with your behavior.

3. Miep Gies risked her life by helping the Annex residents. Describe a time that you have stood up for someone else, or when someone else has stood up for you. Or when you wish you had, but didn't. What would you do differently if you had the chance?

INDEX